INDONESIA
AND JAKARTA

LOUISE SPILSBURY

FRANKLIN WATTS
LONDON•SYDNEY

DEVELOPING WORLD

INDONESIA
AND JAKARTA

W
FRANKLIN WATTS
LONDON • SYDNEY

First published in 2014 by
Franklin Watts
338 Euston Road
London
NW1 3BH

Franklin Watts Australia
Level 17/207 Kent Street
Sydney
NSW 2000

HB ISBN 978 1 4451 2364 6
eBook ISBN 978 14451 2370 7

Dewey number: 915.98

A CIP catalogue record for this book is
available from the British Library.

Series Editor: Julia Bird
Series Advisor: Emma Epsley, geography teacher and consultant
Series Design: sprout.uk.com

Picture credits:
Christopher Beauchamp/Corbis: 43b. Beawiharta/Reuters/Corbis: 40.
Vince Bevan/Alamy: 19b.Caro/Alamy: 42. Corbis: 23. Ethan Daniels/Shutterstock: 30.
Distinctive Images/Shutterstock: 33b. Fandy Djayasputra/Dreamstime: 14. Mikhail Dudarev/Shutterstock: 6.
Matthew Williams Ellis/Robert Harding PL: 31t. EPA/Alamy: 22. Tiago Jorge da Silva Estima/Shutterstock: 37t.
Ngarta Februana/Dreamstime: 17tr, 27tr. Herianius/istockphoto: 12, 17br.
imagemaker/Shutterstock: 18. Images & Stories/Alamy: 36. Joyful/Shutterstock: 32.
JTB Media Creation/Alamy: 34. Keystone USA/ZUMA/Rex Features: 31b.
Olga Khoroshunova/Shutterstock: 11br, 37b. Kzenon /Shutterstock: 38.
Davor Lorincii/istockphoto: 27cl. Edmund Lowe Photography/Shutterstock: 43t.
Minyun9260/Dreamstime: front cover t, 3t. Randy Miramontez/Shutterstock: 35b.
Mosista/Shutterstock: 17tl. Nmedia /Dreamstime: 28. Ocean/Corbis: 41t. Tyler Olson/Shutterstock: 29t.
Crack Palinggi/Reuters/Corbis: 26. Picturepoint/Topham: 8. Paul Prescott/Shutterstock: 41b.
Project 1 Photography/Dreamstime: 15t. christian r/wikimedia commons: 11bl. Ranamaya/Shutterstock: 11t.
rc photo/istockphoto: 15b. Z Ryzner/Shutterstock: 16. saiko3p/Shutterstock: 35t. Valery Shanin/Dreamstime: 33t.
Sipa Press/Rex Features: 19t. Peter Sobolev/Dreamstime: 39b. Sean Sprague/Still Pictures/Robert Harding PL: 21.
Friedrich Stark/Alamy: 20. Peter Stroh/Alamy: 27b. Tatan Syuflana/AP/PAI: 24. Szefei/Shutterstock: 7c. Aleksandar Todrovic/
Shutterstock: 10. Topfoto: 9. United Archives Gmbh/Alamy: front cover b, 3b. wandee0071/Shutterstock: 39t. Tan Kian
Yong/Dreamstime: 25. Zuma Press/Alamy: 13. Zuma Press/Rex Features: 27tl.

Printed in Malaysia

Franklin Watts is a division of
Hachette Children's Books,
an Hachette UK company.
www.hachette.co.uk

INDONESIA
AND JAKARTA

CONTENTS

INDONESIA

Indonesia is a vast and varied country, the biggest in Southeast Asia. It is a land of wild rainforest and isolated tribes, but also of tourist beaches, busy city streets and huge plantations that grow rubber and other materials in demand all over the world.

ENORMOUS COUNTRY

The Indonesian archipelago is made up of more than 13,000 islands, 7,000 or more of which are uninhabited. It sprawls over 5,000 km from east to west. It lies on the equator, which means it has a tropical climate with warm, humid weather all year round.

RAINFOREST AND FARMLAND

Over 60 per cent of Indonesia is covered in thick tropical rainforest, which supports a huge range of plants and wildlife, many of which aren't found anywhere else in the world. However, much of this rainforest has been taken over to provide land for agriculture. Indonesia has rich, fertile soil. This is partly because of its location in the Pacific Ring of Fire (see box). Almost half of all Indonesians work in agriculture, and staple crops include rice, cassava and corn.

Lush rice fields on the Indonesian island of Bali.

DESTRUCTIVE EARTH

Indonesia lies on the Ring of Fire which roughly circles the Pacific Ocean. Here massive rock plates push against or slide past each other, causing earthquakes and forming volcanoes. Indonesia has around 130 active volcanoes, some of which are erupting continuously, and is struck by hundreds of earthquakes each year. On 26 December 2004 an earthquake deep under the Indian Ocean created a huge tsunami which struck the Indonesia province of Aceh, killing over 100,000 people and making over half a million people homeless.

Bangkok

CAMBODIA

VIETNAM

South China Sea

GREATER SUNDA ISLANDS

PHILIPPINES

THAILAND

anda Aceh

Medan Kuala Lumpur

SINGAPORE

Singapore

BRUNEI

MALAYSIA

PACIFIC OCEAN

EQUATOR

Sumatra

Bangka

Kalimantan

Sulawesi

INDONESIA

MALAKU ISLANDS

Papua

PAPUA NEW GUINEA

GREATER SUNDA ISLANDS

Sunda Straits Jakarta

Bandung Java Subaraya Lombok

Yogyakarta Bali Flores

Denpasar

INDIAN OCEAN LESSER SUNDA ISLANDS

EAST TIMOR

AUSTRALIA

TOWNS AND CITIES

Over half of Indonesians live in the country's expanding towns and cities. Many of these are located near the coasts, such as Indonesia's capital city Jakarta and the major port city of Surabaya, which are both well situated for coastal trade.

SPOTLIGHT ON INDONESIA

AREA: 1,904,569 km² • POPULATION: 251,160,124 (2013)

CAPITAL CITY: Jakarta (population: 10 million) • HIGHEST POINT: Puncak Jaya, Irian Jaya, 4,884 m • NUMBER OF ISLANDS: 13,667; 6,000 inhabited • LONGEST RIVER: Kapuas River (1,143 km) •

NATURAL RESOURCES: petroleum, tin, coal, timber, gold

INDONESIA
IN THE PAST

Indonesia has only been an independent country for around 60 years. Over 1,000 years ago the country was a loose collection of Buddhist and Hindu kingdoms dotted across the islands, each with a different local leader. In the 16th century Portuguese traders captured the Malaku Islands to the east of Indonesia. Spices such as nutmeg and cloves that grew in the islands were valuable and in demand in Europe.

DUTCH TRADERS

In the late 16th century Dutch traders representing the powerful Dutch East India Company arrived in Indonesia, drove out the Portuguese and took over territory across the islands. They did this to benefit from Indonesia's rich natural resources, including spices, but also to control the shipping routes in and around the country.

The Dutch East India Company headquarters at Batavia, later to become Jakarta.

INDEPENDENCE

The Dutch ruled Indonesia until the Second World War, when the Japanese briefly occupied the islands. After the Second World War ended, the vast majority of Indonesians wanted an end to Dutch rule. Nationalist leaders including Kusno Sukarno seized the chance to declare independence in 1945. Indonesia was ruled by Sukarno and then his former military leader, General Suharto, for several decades. In that time the economy expanded quickly, boosted by money made from the sale of oil.

INDONESIA TODAY

Indonesia has developed rapidly in recent decades to become the biggest economy in Southeast Asia. During the global economic crisis early in the 21st century it was one of the few countries to keep growing economically. It has a booming export trade based around Indonesia's natural resources, such as rubber, but also has a strong manufacturing industry. Many Indonesians are seeing the benefits of their country's growth – Indonesia has the fastest growing number of millionaires in the world. Yet the majority of its population remains poor, with limited educational opportunities and little access to jobs paying decent wages.

President Sukarno arrives in Jakarta in 1949 for the official transfer of sovereignty from the Netherlands to Indonesia.

FOCUS ON: JAKARTA

The first people to settle on the site of modern day Jakarta chose it for two main reasons. It was located at the mouth of a river, which provided settlers with plenty of fresh water and allowed the easy transport of goods from inland. The location also had a sheltered coast, ideal for docking ships.

PEPPER PORT

By the 13th century the port of Sunda Kelapa, located in the north of present day Jakarta, was an important part of the Sunda kingdom that traded throughout Southeast Asia and China. High quality black pepper, grown in the hills above Sunda, was in particular demand. In 1513 Portuguese traders arrived in Sunda. The rulers of the city offered them land to build a fort and plenty of black pepper in return for protection from other kingdoms. But within a few decades the Portuguese had been defeated, as a rival kingdom took Sunda Kelapa and renamed it Jayakarta.

BATAVIA

At the end of the 16th century Dutch ships started to arrive in Jayakarta in search of riches from the spice trade. City leaders made trading agreements with the Dutch, but also with English traders in the area. Tensions rose and, in 1619, strengthened Dutch forces defeated both the rulers of Jayakarta and the English. They burned down much of the old city and built a new, larger one called Batavia.

Batavia was a walled city similar to many Dutch towns of the era, with canals running through its centre. It had many grand buildings, such as the headquarters of the Dutch East India Company. As Batavia's population grew, the Dutch expanded the city by draining marshlands and clearing forest.

MODERN JAKARTA

In 1949 Batavia was renamed Djakarta or Jakarta as the capital of a fully independent Indonesia. President Sukarno's aim was to transform the capital into a modern city to rival others worldwide. He used state money and encouraged foreign investment to build a grand boulevard, highways, shopping centres, big hotels and high-rise office towers. Later leaders also supported growth and further expansion of the city. Jakarta has grown so much that it has merged with nearby towns to form the 11th largest urban conglomeration in the world, with around 28 million inhabitants.

This old Dutch colonial building in Jakarta is now the Sejarah History Museum.

The high-rise modern buildings of Jakarta sit side-by-side with more traditional buildings.

The National Monument in central Jakarta symbolises the country's struggle for independence.

Jakarta's Mangga Dua Mall is the city's biggest shopping complex.

11

DIVERSE PEOPLES

DIVERSE PEOPLES

Indonesia is home to around 251 million people. The Indonesian population is larger than that of any other country in Southeast Asia, and all the other countries in the world apart from India, the USA and China. The national motto of Indonesia is 'Bhinneka Tunggal Ika' or 'Unity in Diversity'. This refers to the fact that it is a single nation made up of many different islands with around 300 different ethnic groups. Each group has its own unique cultural identity, which can include a distinct language, rituals, ceremonies and celebrations.

JAVANESE AND SUNDANESE

A third of Indonesians are part of the Javan ethnic group. Most live in central and eastern Java in densely populated agricultural regions. The city of Yogyakarta is especially important to Javan culture as it was once capital of the largest Indonesian kingdom. It still retains a sultan as its traditional and cultural, but not political, leader. The second largest group, the Sundanese, also live mostly on Java, but smaller ethnic groups live on other islands, such as the Dayaks of Kalimantan, the Bataks of Sumatra and the Asmat of Papua.

Dayaks buy and sell wares at a floating market in south Borneo.

BISA BICARA BAHASA INDONESIA?

That means 'Do you speak the language *(Bahasa)* of Indonesia?' Most Indonesians do because it is the country's official language. It grew popular nationwide partly because it is not associated more strongly with one ethnic group than any other. However, people often still use the language of their own ethnic group when speaking with family members, especially older ones.

IMMIGRATION

One per cent of Indonesians are of Chinese descent. Their ancestors moved to the region in colonial times. Many acted as trading intermediaries between locals and the Dutch. Some became rich and powerful. This led to jealousy, mistrust and persecution, ranging from massacres of Chinese people through to official bans on Chinese language and exclusion from government or military jobs. Today prejudice is far less – there are even high-profile Chinese Indonesian politicians such as Basuki, lieutenant Governor of Jakarta.

TRANSMIGRATION

In the 1980s the Indonesian government introduced a policy of transmigration. It encouraged poorer people on overcrowded islands such as Java to move to emptier islands by offering them land, money and fertiliser. But one consequence was ethnic tensions between incoming people and groups already living there. In 1996 in Kalimantan 300 people died in clashes between local Dayak people and transmigrated Maduran people.

Schoolchildren dressed in red celebrate Chinese New Year in Java. In the past such displays would most likely have been banned.

POPULATION CHANGES

BIRTH RATE

Indonesia's population has quadrupled in the last eighty years, from 60 million in 1930 to over 250 million in 2010. However, the rate of growth is now slowing down as Indonesians are having fewer children. The average number of children per mother used to be five, but today it is two. This is partly due to a widespread change in people's work, as fewer people are farmers. In agriculture, big families were always seen as desirable as they could help on the farm. The birth rate is also falling because of the promotion of contraception in Indonesia, starting in the 1960s. More children survive past infancy now, owing to improving healthcare in the country. One outcome of fewer children being born and better healthcare is that Indonesians are living longer and the average age of the population is increasing. Over 40 per cent of Indonesians are aged 25–54.

URBANISATION

In the 1950s, only 12 per cent of Indonesians lived in urban areas, but it is predicted that this will rise to over 50 per cent in 2015. This massive shift has happened because of a variety of factors, including the availability of jobs, as the steady growth of urban industries requires more workers. Lower wages and poorer standards of living in rural areas, as well as a lack of farmland in villages, have also contributed to Indonesia's urbanisation. However, there are problems resulting from this trend. At a national scale, Indonesia is struggling to produce the food its people need as there are fewer farmers. At an individual scale, people living in overpopulated cities can experience a shortage of housing, and cramped, polluted conditions.

An aerial view of the sprawling city of Jakarta.

These traditional village houses in Borneo are built on stilts to avoid flooding when river levels rise after rains.

The size of families in Indonesia is shrinking, with just one or two children per family becoming increasingly the norm.

VILLAGE CHANGES

Some Indonesians still live in traditional villages that have changed little for generations. In Kalimantan, some Dayak people still work in agriculture and live in traditional longhouses containing many families' sleeping spaces with communal areas. Yet many others live in modern, private village houses built for single families. Some Indonesians undergo circular migration between village and town life. For example, in Java people may live and work in cities for periods of up to six months and send money home to families or relatives. They return home to live and work for shorter periods during farm harvest periods.

POPULATION STATISTICS

INDONESIA

AVERAGE AGE: 28.5

POPULATION GROWTH RATE: 1%

BIRTH RATE PER 1,000 PEOPLE: 18

AVERAGE NUMBER OF CHILDREN PER MOTHER: 2

INFANT DEATH RATE PER 1,000 BIRTHS: 27

LIFE EXPECTANCY: 71

FOCUS ON: JAKARTA

BUSY CITY

Jakarta is one of the most crowded cities in the world, with population density of around 14,000 people per km². It is growing faster than the rest of Indonesia because so many people migrate to the city to find work. This overcrowding adversely affects life in the capital in many ways – Jakarta is low down the list of 'best cities to live in', ranked 125 out of 140.

HOUSING SHORTAGES

Some *Batawi* (residents of Jakarta) live in gated luxury houses or in high-rise blocks, but most cannot afford to buy or rent such homes. They live in slums called *kampungs* and other illegal settlements, or in cheaper homes in the sprawling metropolitan area.

TRANSPORT

Millions of people commute to work each day, and public transport is limited. Trains are often so full that people have to ride on the roof! As a result of poor public transport and increasing wealth, more Batawi are choosing to drive to work, resulting in daily traffic jams, and poor air quality. The economic costs of health problems and lost working hours are estimated at around US$5 billion each year. The growth of car ownership is also placing a strain on Jakarta's roads. Many roads are inadequate for their use or in disrepair. In 2010 a 100-metre section of four-lane highway collapsed into a river in north Jakarta.

FLOODS AND SANITATION

Jakarta regularly floods in the rainy season. Such is the demand for land to build on that it has few parks and marshland areas that can absorb floodwater. Drainage is slow as the River Ciliwung and canals are blocked with waste, often from kampungs along their banks. Most people, except those in slums, have piped water but sanitation is often poor. Most sewage goes straight into the river, where the poorest also wash.

SOLUTIONS

The government is making or considering making improvements to living conditions in Jakarta in many ways. The Kampung Improvement Programme is an ongoing government scheme to improve housing quality and access to sanitation. Public transport congestion will be eased by the construction of the Jakarta metro, expected to be complete by 2016. In the meantime, the government has introduced fines for people who drive into the city without passengers. However, 'jockeys' are on the rise – people whom single drivers pay to get in their car for less than the cost of the fine!

A riverside slum or kampung near the business district of central Jakarta. An estimated 25 per cent of residents live in slum settlements like these.

Young passengers ride on the rooftop of a commuter train in Jakarta.

These modern Jakartan apartment blocks offer better living conditions, but are beyond the reach of many of Jakarta's poorer residents.

Jakarta's roads are often heavily congested.

GOVERNING INDONESIA

GENERAL SUHARTO

Indonesia is a democratic republic – a group of separate, independent parts ruled centrally by an elected leader. The longest serving president of Indonesia was Suharto, who overthrew President Sukarno in a bloody military coup in 1968. His government gave the country political stability, which helped its economic development, but was authoritarian and repressive. Suharto and his family were also believed to have too much power, as they controlled the country's banks, as well as the lucrative petrol industry.

A NEW DEMOCRACY

In the mid-1990s an economic crisis in Asia meant many Indonesians became poorer. There were riots and protests against Suharto, leading him to resign in 1998. Since the end of Suharto's rule, Indonesia's presidents have become more democratic, for example by increasing freedom of speech and negotiating the end to conflicts over government rule in East Timor and Aceh (see box). President Susilo Bambang Yudhoyono has been in power since 2004.

NATIONAL AND REGIONAL GOVERNMENT

Yudhoyono is the leader of Indonesia's parliament, which is called the People's Consultative Assembly. It is made up of politicians elected within the 30 administrative provinces, two special regions (Aceh and Yogyakarta) and the capital city district, Jakarta. Their job is to debate and determine state policies and laws. Within each province there are district and city leaders who control local government – anything from town planning to providing refuse collection or a fire service.

Susilo Bambang Yudhoyono (right) was re-elected President of Indonesia in 2009 for another five year term.

WOMEN IN POLITICS

In 2009 a law was passed stating that each political party must have at least 30 per cent female candidates for Parliament, but this figure has yet to be reached and is still only about 18 per cent. Increasing the political power of women is important for Indonesia as it can help reduce gender inequality in other areas. For example, women make up 45 per cent of the civil service workforce, but only nine per cent of those are in positions of power, and literacy rates remain lower for women than for men.

Inside Indonesia's parliament building in Jakarta.

EAST TIMOR

Timor is an island which was colonised in the 16th and 17th centuries by Portugal in the west and the Dutch in the east. At independence in 1949, West Timor became part of Indonesia, but Portugal retained East Timor until 1974. In 1975, Suharto's army invaded and took over East Timor. This started a long conflict in which thousands of Timorese died. There was an international outcry at Indonesia's military aggression and support for East Timorese freedom. In 2002 East Timor became a separate country.

Armed guerillas in East Timor fought government troops for decades over the independence of their homeland.

EDUCATION
AND HEALTH

GOING TO SCHOOL

Education is compulsory in Indonesia from the age of 7 to 13 at elementary school, and 13 to 15 at secondary school. At elementary school children learn the national language of Bahasa Indonesia, maths, religion, nationalism (the history and culture of their country), art and sports. Science is introduced at secondary school. After compulsory education, some families pay to enrol their children for three more years at secondary school. Around 11 per cent of young people go on to college or university.

MISSING OUT

Indonesia spends around 17 per cent of its budget on education and has achieved 90 per cent literacy. However, around 2.5 million children, mostly 13–15-year olds, who should be in school, are not. Poor children are more likely to miss school. In rural areas, children may drop out to work on family farms. Girls often drop out to help look after younger siblings. The charity UNICEF is working with communities to monitor attendance at schools and educate families about the importance of education.

Many think that Indonesian children should be able to learn in the language of their ethnic group to help them learn faster and get better grades.

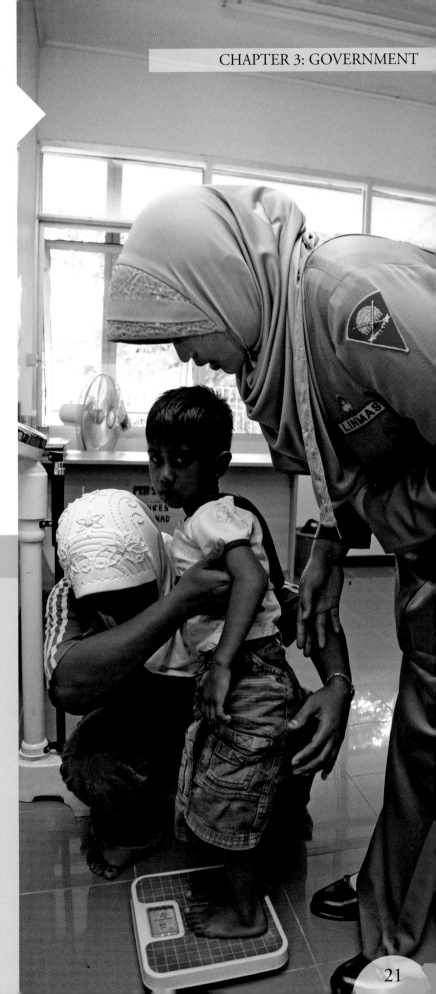

A healthcare worker weighs a child as part of a screening at a village health centre.

HEALTHCARE

Indonesia has a national healthcare network that offers free or cheap basic treatment at district medical centres, rural community and village health centres called *puskesmas* and small health posts throughout the country. However, many Indonesians who live outside of the major cities struggle to get more specialised healthcare. One factor is the cost, but another is a lack of trained medical workers. The Indonesian government is trying to change this by requiring medical graduates to work for a year in rural areas. However, few stay on beyond this minimum term.

MIDWIVES & MILK

In the past, many Indonesian babies died at birth. Today the infant mortality rate is lower, mainly because the government has invested in intensive training for local midwives. However, some midwives get rewards such as TVs or money for encouraging mothers to feed formula milk to their babies. When mixed with clean water and used properly, formula milk powder can be as good for babies as breastmilk. But in a country where some mothers have little education and 45% of people have no access to clean water, its promotion can be dangerous.

21

CORRUPTION

In 2013 Ana Urbaningram (centre) resigned as the chairman of the ruling Democratic Party in Indonesia. It was alleged he took bribes relating to the construction of a sports complex.

POLITICS

Corruption is a big issue in Indonesia – anything from paying a policeman to overlook a speeding ticket to bribing officials to unload goods at a port faster is often considered a normal part of life. So widespread is the problem that even government officials often award lucrative contracts to companies in return for hefty bribes. In 2012 a third of 470 regional head politicians had been found guilty of different types of corruption, and many others, including President Yudhoyono, were suspected of it. Apart from receiving bribes, politicians sometimes embezzle state money for themselves or their political parties, and even bribe people to vote for them in elections.

HARMFUL IMPACTS

Corruption is harmful to democracy, as people can lose faith in the politicians they have elected, and it is unfair on the poorest people who cannot afford bribes. It is also harming Indonesia in other ways. For example, in 2011 a major bridge collapsed in Kalimantan, killing 18 people. It had been poorly built and maintained by contractors whom, it was alleged, had only got the work because they had bribed officials. Corruption can also hamper development, as companies hoping to invest money in Indonesia may be put off by corruption.

Protestors outside the Anti-Corruption Agency in Jakarta display uniforms which they want people accused of corruption to wear when they appear in court.

STOPPING CORRUPTION

Komisi Pemberantasan Korupsi (KPK) is the government law-enforcement body which was set up in 2003 to fight corruption in Indonesia. The KPK has proven the guilt of many corrupt politicians and recovered billions of dollars of bribes and other payments they received. But work is slow because the KPK has just 700 employees investigating corruption on a massive scale.

The KPK also helps educate people about corruption. It produces anti-corruption modules for teaching at school and promotes 'Honesty Shops' in schools where pupils pay for what they take by putting money in a box, rather than paying a cashier. The KPK's anti-corruption message is spreading nationally and people across Indonesia are increasingly voting against politicians who are corrupt.

A GROWING ECONOMY

SUCCESS STORY

Indonesia has the 16th biggest economy in the world. It is growing at a rate of around six per cent each year while growth in other, more developed, economies is slowing or stalling. It is growing partly because Indonesia's abundant natural resources are in great demand internationally. As the economy strengthens, more Indonesians are wealthy enough to buy new products, from cars to fridges, boosting the economy still further. These factors are encouraging foreign investors, such as Chinese banks, to invest around £14 billion a year in Indonesia to help set up new industries.

TRADE

In the past, Indonesia mostly exported foods, rubber, timber and metals such as tin. Raw materials such as coal, petrol, natural gas and minerals are still major exports today. But part of the country's economic development has been achieved by expanding its manufacturing industries to produce goods for export. These range from sheet materials made from tropical timber, used in construction, to electrical goods, shoes and clothing. Indonesia trades almost exclusively with other Asian countries, but also the USA. It imports the things it does not produce domestically from countries such as China and Singapore. These include machinery, chemicals and foods (see box).

Busy container ports are a key part of the export trade that the country relies on for its economic development.

WORKFORCE

There are over 115 million people in the Indonesian workforce, but there are widely varying wages between the top and bottom earners. The poorest, working in informal jobs (see page 26) earn as little as £1 per day. Most Indonesians work in the service industry, serving in shops, banks or working in the country's tourist industry. Just 12 per cent of the working population work in industry, such as in textile factories or mines, but they produce nearly half of Indonesia's GDP. Around six per cent of Indonesians who are able to work are unemployed.

OCCUPATION BY SECTOR

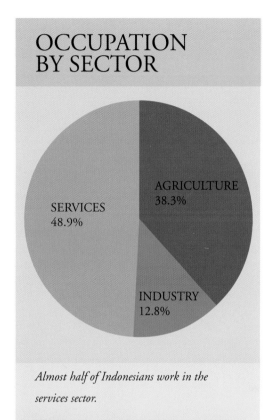

SERVICES
48.9%

AGRICULTURE
38.3%

INDUSTRY
12.8%

Almost half of Indonesians work in the services sector.

A tractor collects crops in an Indonesian oil palm plantation.

FOOD SECURITY

Despite its large agricultural sector, Indonesia does not produce enough food for its population. It needs to import much of its staple food, rice, as well as beef, soya beans and wheat. This is because only 18 per cent of its land is farmland. Large parts of this grow cash crops for export, including soya and palm oil. Palm oil is widely used in processed foods including margarine, and in cosmetics. It is also increasingly used as a type of biofuel (see page 39).

FOCUS ON: JAKARTA

BATAWI WORKERS

Around two of the five million working Batawi have jobs in Jakarta's service and manufacturing industries. These range from jobs in banks and insurance companies, hotel groups and stores in central Jakarta to working in electronics, automotive, chemical, mechanical engineering, textile and biomedical factories in other parts of the city. Most factories and plants are located on the outskirts of Jakarta, in new industrial parks.

THE INFORMAL SECTOR

Other Batawi have informal jobs with no employment contracts. They often run their own small businesses and wages vary day to day. Around a quarter run or work in small restaurants called *warung*. Others own small businesses such as motorcycle taxi services, TV repair shops or tiny stores called *tokos* which sell basic household supplies. Some informal workers are street vendors who sell items such as food and toys from carts. Others find work as maids or construction workers.

LOOKING FORWARD

The population of Jakarta is growing faster than the number of well-paid jobs, so many workers are forced to work for low wages and in poor working conditions. For example, in large sportswear factories workers are often forced to work a 65-hour week, earning as little as 30 pence a day. However, the Jakarta regional government is trying to improve working opportunities and conditions for its people. It provides five vocational training centres in the city. These offer courses and certificates for computer operators, electricians, English language teachers and other vocations. The minimum working wage was also increased by 44 per cent in 2012, and the government is working hard to make sure that people actually receive this.

This new Honda factory near Jakarta produces over 100,000 new vehicles each year for the Indonesian market.

Women at work at Sritex textile factory in Jakarta.

A fruit seller in central Jakarta.

Even poor Batawi eat out in warungs because prices are low and it is often cheaper than buying food themselves.

Rubbish collectors screen newly arrived waste at a Jakarta rubbish tip for plastic bottles, metal and other things they can sell.

27

TRANSPORT AND INFRASTRUCTURE

ON THE ROAD

Indonesia has an established transport network of shipping, airlines, roads and some railways, mostly located on the island of Java. Most Indonesians use road transport. Trucks carry most freight and people travel using anything from rickshaws and mopeds to intercity buses. Car ownership is low, but rising fast. There are around 60 private cars per 1,000 people, but in 2012 car sales were 25 per cent higher than in 2011.

Farm labourers in Java cycling to work in nearby rice fields.

KEY SERVICES

Indonesia's infrastructure is often inadequate. Only around half of its roads are paved, and they are found mostly on Java, Sumatra and Bali. The country is not yet able to provide enough electricity to industries and consumers, and there are often power blackouts several times a week. Water infrastructure is also inadequate in large parts of Indonesia. Many dams and reservoirs have limited capacity to store the country's abundant rainfall owing to filling with sediment from farmland, and there are too few water processing plants to supply the growing population of Indonesia.

ONLINE

National and international e-commerce is currently limited as only around 20 per cent of Indonesians have Internet accounts, although many others use Internet cafes and, increasingly, mobile smartphones.

IMPROVEMENTS

The Indonesian government has a plan of infrastructure development. It plans to spend £4 billion on upgrading airports, ports and fishery production facilities in Nusa Tenggara (including Bali) to improve tourism and food production, and £40 billion on improving Kalimantan as a centre for production and processing of mining and energy. The biggest single infrastructure project is the 30-kilometre Sunda Straits Bridge, linking Java and Sumatra (see box).

Roads in more remote, less populated places are made from compacted mud and can be washed away in heavy rain.

An artist's impression of how the Sunda Straits Bridge will look once it is complete.

VIEWS ON A BRIDGE

The Sunda Straits Bridge is a controversial project. On the one hand, it will increase trade between the islands. Transport by bridge is faster and safer than ships in the busy, dangerous waters of the Straits.

'When Java and Sumatra are connected by the bridge, the flow of goods and energy between the two islands will become faster and smoother.'
(R. Sukhyar, Energy and Mineral Resources Ministry, Sumatra)

On the other, opponents say the high estimated cost of £19 billion could improve infrastructure across Indonesia, not just on the two islands that are already most developed. And the bridge is very near Krakatau volcano.

'This money is enough to build 90,000 schools or … 22,500 km … of high-speed railway [connecting] all major cities in Indonesia… The bridge will join Sumatra and Java but, on the flip side, it has great potential to disjoint the nation.'
(Wijayanto, Vice-rector of Paramadina University, 2012)

TOURISM

A GROWTH INDUSTRY

Tourism is an important and fast-growing element of the service industry in Indonesia. There were around eight million foreign arrivals in Indonesia in 2013, a million more than in 2010, and these visitors spent around £6 billion on their travels. Some people travel to Indonesia to do business, but many others are in Indonesia as tourists. All use local services, from banks and restaurants to shops and tour guides, during their stay.

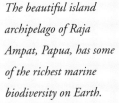

The beautiful island archipelago of Raja Ampat, Papua, has some of the richest marine biodiversity on Earth.

DESTINATIONS

Most foreign visitors are from nearby Malaysia, Singapore and Australia, and over a third of all arrivals land at Bali airport. Bali is renowned for its beautiful beaches and distinctive culture. It also has well-developed tourism facilities, a range of accommodation and good roads for getting around. Many other parts of Indonesia have a wealth of tourist attractions, ranging from the giant Komodo dragon lizards in Nusa Tenggara to forest and tropical bays in Papua, but are less visited as they are less developed and often more difficult to reach.

CHALLENGES

Neighbouring Malaysia is much smaller than Indonesia, but has many more tourists, partly because it has better infrastructure. Indonesia has a reputation as a challenging destination for several reasons. Poor infrastructure makes travel slow and unpredictable, and means that tourist amenities vary a lot in quality. Indonesia also has a reputation for being unsafe to travel in some areas. Tourism dipped after terrorists bombed a Bali nightclub in 2002, and the British Foreign Office advises caution in Aceh where a British tourist was abducted in June 2013.

Tourists pay their respects at a memorial commemorating the victims of the Bali nightclub bombings.

HAPPY TRAVELS

Ecotourism balances the needs of tourists with conservation of the environment and respecting local cultures. It is one of the fastest growing sectors in the tourism industry in Indonesia. The Rinjani Trekking Center in Lombok, for example, offers tours up the sacred volcano, Gunung Rinjani. It employs local guides with good knowledge of local mountain conditions. They ensure that visitors leave no litter and don't disturb local wildlife. Over half of the entrance fee into Rinjani National Park goes to the trekking centre's work. There are ecotourism projects across Indonesia, from Bali to Kalimantan, many given financial support not just by Indonesia, but also by foreign investors. For example, the Flores tourism organisation is partly funded by a Swiss development organisation.

RELIGION

A colourful procession of giant models of demons marks the Hindu festival of Nyepi in Ubud, Bali. The monsters symbolise evil spirits which people believe should be expelled from their lives.

MAJOR FAITHS

Islam first arrived in Indonesia in the 13th century when Arab traders visited the islands. Today, around 200 million Indonesians follow Islam, making it the largest Muslim nation in the world. Islam is especially dominant in areas such as Aceh, western Sumatra and western Java. The government legally recognises just five religions other than Islam – Protestantism, Catholicism, Hinduism, Buddhism and Confucianism. Christianity is commonest in areas including Flores, West Timor and Celebes where Christian missionaries were active, while most locals on Bali are Hindu. The main followers of Buddhism and Confucianism are Indonesians of Chinese descent.

RELIGIOUS INTOLERANCE

During the recent economic development, some Muslims have reacted against growing signs of wealth, luxuries and more liberal, modern behaviour in Indonesia. They have become more orthodox in their views. In some areas this has led to a spread of shari'a law – a legal system controlled by religious leaders that influences many aspects of life, such as dress and behaviour, and advocates harsh punishments for criminals. Orthodox beliefs have led to increasing intolerance of other faiths in Indonesia in some areas.

Many Batak people living in north Sumatra, Indonesia, are Christian. This is the Batak Christian Church on Samosir Island, Sumatra.

AHMIDAYYAH

Indonesians belonging to any of Indonesia's non-recognised religions sometimes face discrimination, such as being refused jobs or being restricted from worshipping. Intolerance can also sometimes spill over into violence. The Ahmidayyah faith is a Muslim sect with beliefs about Muhammad that are not tolerated by orthodox Muslims. Ahmidayyah is restricted or banned in many places, especially in western Java. In 2011 three Ahmadiyyah worshippers were beaten to death by a mob, and in 2013 three Ahmidayyah mosques were damaged and closed down by local residents.

Young Muslims study their holy book, the Qur'an.

THE ARTS

TRADITIONAL ARTS

Traditional arts remain popular in parts of Indonesia. One of the most famous forms is *wayang kulit* or shadow puppets, which create intricate silhouettes on a screen. Wayang kulit are used to perform plays based on Hindu epic poems, such as the *Mahabharata,* and feature famous characters from Hindu mythology. These traditional plays can last for over ten hours, during which audience members come and go.

In wayang kulit shows a puppet master and helpers move leather puppets using sticks in front of a lamp, creating shadows on a screen for the audience on the other side to see.

GAMELAN

A gamelan is a percussion instrument orchestra found in Java and Bali. It uses brass gongs, glockenspiels and drums. The haunting, rhythmic music played by gamelans has developed out of a blend of Chinese, Indian, Middle Eastern and European influences. The music is often heard accompanying religious rituals. Gamelan music is changing with the influence of western music, however. For example, some gamelans now perform alongside drums, keyboard and guitars typical of US pop music.

Musicians in a gamelan play traditional Balinese music to accompany dancers in Ubud, Bali.

TV AND SOCIAL MEDIA

Indonesia has many national TV stations of its own and receives programmes by satellite and cable from other countries. One of the most popular Indonesian stations is Indosiar. Some of its programmes, such as shadow puppet performances, attract older audiences. Others such as Asian dramas showing young, successful, urban characters, talent competitions and reality shows, including a dating show called 'Take Me Out Indonesia', are more popular amongst younger audiences. As the country develops digitally, younger Indonesians also increasingly use social media to see daily news, interact with networks of other people both nationally and internationally, and share cultural preferences and ideas. Indonesia was the third highest country for Facebook use in the world in 2012.

NEW MUSIC

Dangdut is a popular form of Indonesian dance music. It has strong rhythms, which are played out on bongo drums. It is influenced by Indian and Malaysian film music, as well as US pop. Another popular style of music is Pop Indonesia. This is heavily influenced not only by US pop, rock and hip-hop, but also by Korean pop acts such as Girls' Generation and PSY, performer of 'Gangnam Style'. Korean music is widely listened to in Indonesia as Korean groups are widely advertised and promoted in the region. These groups, some of which were created in talent shows on Korean TV, are among the most popular amongst Indonesian teenagers.

The Asian girl group Blush was created live on satellite TV. They have won a devoted following in Indonesia and Singapore.

DEFORESTATION

UNDER THREAT

Indonesia has the third largest area of tropical rainforest in the world. It is believed to be home to 10 per cent of all the world's known plant species, 12 per cent of mammal species and 17 per cent of bird species. But Indonesia's forests are disappearing fast. By the early 21st century an area about the size of Wales was being cleared each year. This has led to a loss of rainforest habitat for Indonesia's rich wildlife. By 2013, Sumatran orangutan populations had dropped by 80 per cent and many other species, including the rare Sumatran tiger and rhino, are now critically endangered.

Deforested, cleared land in Sulawesi, Indonesia. Most forest is cleared – often by burning – for agriculture and logging.

IMPACTS

Destroying tropical rainforest has many effects, including loss of biodiversity. Forest trees suck up water and release water vapour, cooling local climates. With no roots to hold together soil, it washes off land to clog rivers, lakes and reservoirs, causing flooding on land. Rainforest trees and plants release oxygen that many living things respire. With fewer trees in Indonesia, local and international climates and atmosphere are affected. Fires to clear land can cause raging forest fires that destroy even more forest. Smoke from these fires mixes with vehicle emissions, especially in cities, creating harmful smog. This affects Indonesia, but also nearby countries. In 2013 the Indonesian government apologised to neighbouring Singapore and Malaysia for air pollution caused by fires clearing forest for oil palm plantations on Sumatra.

VITAL STATS

AREA OF FOREST: 94.5 million hectares or 52% of total land area

PRIMARY FOREST: 50% of forest area

ILLEGAL LOGGING: around 75% of all timber logged in Indonesia

THREATENED SPECIES: 772, third highest in the world after the USA and Malaysia

The last of Indonesia's tigers live on Sumatra in tropical forest and swamplands. Loss of habitat and hunting has reduced their population to around 400.

PRIVATE ACTION

Individuals and companies can take action against rainforest destruction by only buying products that have certificates confirming they are not sourced from Indonesian primary forests. In 2012 the environmental charity Greenpeace discovered that APP, the third largest paper company in the world, made paper containing endangered tree species from protected areas. After negative publicity for APP several major office suppliers, including Xerox, stopped buying its paper. In 2013 APP announced that it would only make paper using wood from plantations or non-primary forest areas.

Rafflesia, which is found in Indonesian primary forest, is the largest single flower in the world, measuring 90 cm across.

GOVERNMENT ACTION

The Indonesian government is trying to make forest development more sustainable – balancing economic benefit from forest resources with preserving the forest environment now and into the future. It has initiated programmes to plant trees on deforested land to increase tree cover, and protects large areas of its primary forest, often in forest reserves. However, even protected forest can be approved for logging by regional governments hoping to create wealth and jobs. In 2013 for instance, the Aceh government planned to approve clearance of 1.2 million hectares for new palm oil plantations. However, most deforestation in Indonesia is illegal and continues even on protected land, owing to corruption and too few government officials to properly monitor forest activity.

POWERING DEVELOPMENT

ENERGY EXPENSE

A lot of energy is needed to power Indonesia's industrial development, and this is having a big impact on the atmosphere. Most electricity in Indonesia is generated in coal-fired power stations. Burning coal and other fossil fuels releases carbon dioxide and other greenhouse gases that contribute to global warming. Carbon dioxide is also being released in Indonesia when deforestation uncovers deep, peat-rich soils that react with oxygen in the air. Carbon dioxide is also given out when trees and peat burn. In 1998 enormous forest fires throughout Indonesia released an amount of carbon dioxide equal to around 40 per cent of the average annual emissions from burning fossil fuels around the world!

Morning sunlight in Jakarta reveals smog and dust surrounding the city buildings and streets.

LOWERING EMISSIONS

In 2011, President Yudhoyono announced a national action plan to reduce greenhouse gas emissions by 26 per cent by 2020. The country already generates around 15 per cent of its power using renewable energy. It is increasing its use of renewable energy by building more hydroelectric and geothermal power stations, and by encouraging the use of solar power in homes. It also plans to encourage Indonesians to be more energy efficient, for example by using energy-saving appliances. Other emission reduction strategies range from better conservation of peat soils to stop them drying and releasing carbon dioxide, and growing rice varieties that release less methane (a greenhouse gas).

RAINFOREST DIESEL

Palm oil plantations are expanding across Indonesia, especially on the deforested, peat-rich soils of Sumatra and Kalimantan. One of the growing uses of palm oil is in the form of biodiesel, which can be used to fuel vehicles. Producing and using biodiesel made from palm oil emits around 15 per cent less carbon dioxide per litre than normal diesel, and it is a renewable energy source, whereas oil supplies worldwide are running out. At present just 12 per cent of palm oil companies in Indonesia produce sustainable palm oil (from plantations not adversely affecting primary forests and local communities). This is set to rise by 2015 when several multinational companies such as Unilever and Walmart have pledged to use only sustainable palm oil.

Harvesting palm oil fruit. The fruit are pressed to produce oil that is then processed into biodiesel.

A geothermal power station in Sumatra. Indonesia's location on the Ring of Fire means that there is great potential to use energy from hot rock not far beneath the Earth's surface.

TIN MINING

SMART TIN

Tin is used worldwide in the manufacture of the electric circuits used in smartphones, tablets and TVs, among other goods. World demand for tin is having a great impact on the small, tin-rich island of Bangka in Indonesia. Indonesia exports more tin than any other country and 90 per cent of this comes from Bangka and nearby Belitung.

GETTING TIN

One in five people on Bangka are tin miners. Some search for rock rich in tin – tin ore – on land, using digging machines or pickaxes. Others suck up or dredge sand containing grains of ore from beaches and the seafloor around the island. Around 40 per cent of people on Bangka work in tin-related jobs, such as processing the ore into tin metal.

Tin mining sites such as this dominate the landscape of Bangka. High-pressure hoses are used to wash tin ore from the soft, sandy rock.

CHALLENGES

The growth in use of electronic devices continues. The number of smartphones in use globally, for example, rose from 700 million in 2011 to 1 billion in 2012. This is predicted to rise to near 8 billion by 2016. The Indonesian government has to balance the economic benefits of its booming tin industry with its costs for places like Bangka. It could start by encouraging tin mining companies to limit dredging and suction mining, not only to conserve delicate marine habitats, but also to protect the fishing industry.

MINING IMPACTS

Mining provides jobs and wealth on Bangka, but is having many negative impacts:

- Pollution: chemicals used to process tin pollute freshwater in rivers and groundwater, harming wildlife, damaging crops and polluting drinking water.

- Deforestation: little forest is left on the island as it has been cleared for mining.

- Fishing industry: damaged reefs and cloudy water make fish live further out to sea. Local fishermen have to travel further and use more fuel to catch fish.

- Loss of reefs: coral reefs thrive in clear water and die when mud produced during mining clouds the water. Over two-thirds of Bangka's reefs are dead.

- Beach destruction: ruined beaches put off tourists and reduce local income.

The tropical islands of Bangka and nearby Belitung lie east of Sumatra.

The fishing industry on Bangka is being wrecked by the impact of tin mining on water quality.

THE FUTURE FOR INDONESIA

ECONOMIC SECURITY

Running a country as vast and scattered as Indonesia is an enormous challenge for any government. Abundant natural resources, booming trade and growing domestic consumption should encourage the growth of its industries. But it may need to manage its reliance on international exports to underpin the economy, as their value can go up and down. During the recent global economic downturn, China's industry produced less and therefore needed to import less coal, which impacted on Indonesia's economy. Rising international prices for palm oil and other cash crops encourage more deforestation and plantation farming, at the expense of sufficient farming of food to meet domestic needs.

A FRESH START FOR JAKARTA?

In 2013 Joko Widodo was elected the new governor of Jakarta. His election campaign focused on improving public transport, housing, wages, flood reduction and clean water supply. He introduced the Jakarta Health Card which provided free access to healthcare that people had previously had to pay for, and the Jakarta Smart Card which supplied a monthly grant for families to spend on school supplies, such as uniforms and books. Such reforms face practical problems. In some hospitals there were 70 per cent more patients than usual, causing overcrowding and even deaths, and expensive social care may need to be funded by higher taxes. But more Batawi feel their government is caring for them than before.

A village meeting between locals and charity Care International over improving water supply and sanitation. Better infrastructure is required across Indonesia if the quality of people's lives is to improve.

ENVIRONMENTAL FUTURE

Indonesia also needs to become more environmentally sustainable in its drive for development. Moderating deforestation is essential for protecting rainforest, but also to ensure a forest resource for the future. The government can help conserve forests by encouraging local people to work sustainably with them, for example through ecotourism or community plantations which can both provide regular income without harming the rainforest. Improved regional development should help to reduce urban overcrowding and relieve pressure on water supply, sanitation and air quality.

Raising and planting tree seedlings to create plantations will ensure a steady supply of trees to log without harming natural forests.

KEEPING THE PEOPLE HAPPY

Some Indonesians are reaping the benefits of their country's economic success, but many are still excluded by poverty. The government needs to ensure that people nationwide, male or female, and regardless of religious beliefs, benefit more evenly from the country's development. One way to do this is to invest more in improving infrastructure, and in providing better education and social welfare, such as healthcare and pensions, for its people. The rising average age of Indonesia's population means that in future there will be increased demand for social welfare. But Indonesians will trust their government to spend its money far better if more real action is taken to fight widespread political corruption.

Rice terraces in Bali. Indonesia's farming industry must balance feeding its population with producing crops for a global market.

GLOSSARY

archipelago cluster or chain of islands in one area of sea

authoritarian when people are forced to strictly obey authority at the expense of personal freedom

Bahasa Indonesia official language of Indonesia, which developed from Malay used by traders in the region in the past

Batawi person from or who lives in Jakarta

biodiversity variety of plant and animal life in a particular habitat or in the world as a whole

cash crop crop grown for direct sale, often for export, and not generally for use by farmers or locals

democratic republic system of government where leaders are elected by the people and where authority is determined by the people, not by inheritance

earthquake violent shaking of ground caused by slabs of rock undergrounds pushing into and rubbing against each other

ecotourism type of tourism that minimises ecological impact or damage and usually promotes the involvement of local people.

embezzle to steal money from an organisation or business that you work for

equator imaginary horizontal line around the centre of the Earth which is an equal distance from each pole. Countries on the equator have sunny weather nearly all year around

ethnic group people with a shared, distinctive culture, language, religion and other beliefs, whose ancestors usually came from a particular place

export to send goods to another country for sale

fossil fuel coal, oil or gas that formed underground over millions of years from the remains of living things

GDP gross domestic product, a measure of the total value of goods and services produced by a country in one year

global economic crisis period starting in 2007 and 2008 when many banks and finance institutions lost money and closed, leading to worldwide economic difficulties for countries, corporations and individuals

global warming rise in worldwide average temperatures caused by increased amounts of gases in the atmosphere trapping more of the Sun's heat. The gases are mostly released by machines and by other human activities

infrastructure essential facilities and structures for public use, from roads and bridges to water pipes and sewage treatment plants

intra-urban within a city or other built-up place

kampung cluster of housing ranging from a small rural village to a shanty town within a city

metropolitan relating to a large city

minerals naturally occurring substance not derived from living things usually obtained or exploited by mining. Minerals range from gold to limestone

palm oil oil from the crushed fruit of particular types of palm trees that grow in tropical countries. Palm oil is used in cooking and foods but also to make vehicle fuel

peat dark soil made from decaying plants found in bogs and swamps. Dried peat can be used as a fuel

photosynthesis natural process that happens in green plants where sugar and oxygen are made from carbon dioxide and water using sunlight

plantation group of trees or other plants planted and managed in order to harvest for sale

rainforest dense forest often with high biodiversity growing in areas with high rainfall, such as tropical countries

renewable resources such as wind, Sun and water which are capable of being renewed and will not run out

repression restraint or suppression, often by force

Ring of Fire zone bordering the Pacific Ocean with a high frequency of earthquakes and volcanoes

service industry collection of companies and organisations that create jobs and wealth without providing goods. Service industries include shops, hotels and transport

Southeast Asia geographical region between India, China, Australia and the Pacific Ocean, which includes countries such as Thailand, Vietnam and Indonesia

staple food food generally eaten as a large part of their diet by a given population to supply basic nutrition, such as rice, maize, wheat or cassava

tsunami destructive, high ocean wave caused by a subsea earthquake.

urban conglomeration group of settlements that have merged into one larger urban unit

urban sprawl uncontrolled spread and expansion of a city or town

urbanisation growth of and migration to cities and towns

rather than rural areas in a country or region

volcano hill or mountain around an opening in the Earth's crust through which molten rock or lava, gases and ash escapes or erupts

FURTHER INFORMATION

BOOKS

Indonesia (Odyssey Passport), Bill Dalton, Odyssey Publications, 2013

We Visit Indonesia (Your Land and My Land: Asia), Tammy Gagne, Mitchell Lane Publishers, 2014

WEBSITES

http://www.undp.or.id/general/about_geography.asp
The United Nations Development Programme site for Indonesia has information about economy, population, climate and more.

http://www.unicef.org/indonesia/reallives_2944.html
Read real-life stories about children and education in Indonesia.

http://ran.org/sites/default/files/indonesia_climatechange_rainforests.pdf
This online booklet has lots about Indonesian rainforests.

http://kids.embassyofindonesia.org/aboutIndonesiahistory.htm
Find out about the history, people, geography and more.

INDEX